Contents

Using This Leader Guide

Before the group meets

- Read the chapter in *You & Your Family* that will be discussed at the next group meeting. Look up all biblical references and answer every question.

- Read through the **Leader Sheet** for the appropriate meeting. Each meeting has three parts—"**Inspect**" (the Bible passages), "**Reflect**" (on the principles drawn from the passages), and "**Connect**" (the principles to daily living). Under each part there are at least two activities from which you can choose. Knowing that each activity will take approximately 10 minutes to complete, you can select those that best fit your group members and the time available.

- Collect all the items listed under "**Materials**." Anything not provided in this guide can be obtained at little or no cost. Group members are expected to bring their own Bibles and pens or pencils. You may wish to keep extras Bibles and sharpened pencils on hand.

- Memorize the chapter theme printed under the **Leader Sheet** title to help you keep the meeting focused.

- Write summaries of the previous meeting's prayer requests under "**Past Needs.**"

With the group

- Greet all group members as they arrive, asking them questions that let them know you are genuinely and personally interested in them.

- Make any announcements before beginning on time with prayer. Consider using the "**Suggested Prayer.**"

- Go through the discussion questions and activities you selected. Gauge time carefully to remain on schedule. Each activity should take approximately 10 minutes.

- If group members arrive after the meeting starts, greet them by name and summarize what the group is doing. Do your best to make them comfortable, not conspicuous.

- Devote the last 10 minutes of meeting time to prayer. Ask group members to share what has happened with the needs recorded under "**Past Needs.**" Ask them to also share any new prayer requests with the group, recording these under "**New Needs.**"

After the group meeting

- Using the **Call Record Sheet**, call every group member in the first few days after each group meeting. Learn how the book and meetings are impacting his or her day-to-day life. Spend half the call building a relationship. End each call with a personal prayer for God's blessing in the group member's life.

- Pray daily for all recorded prayer requests and for every group member.

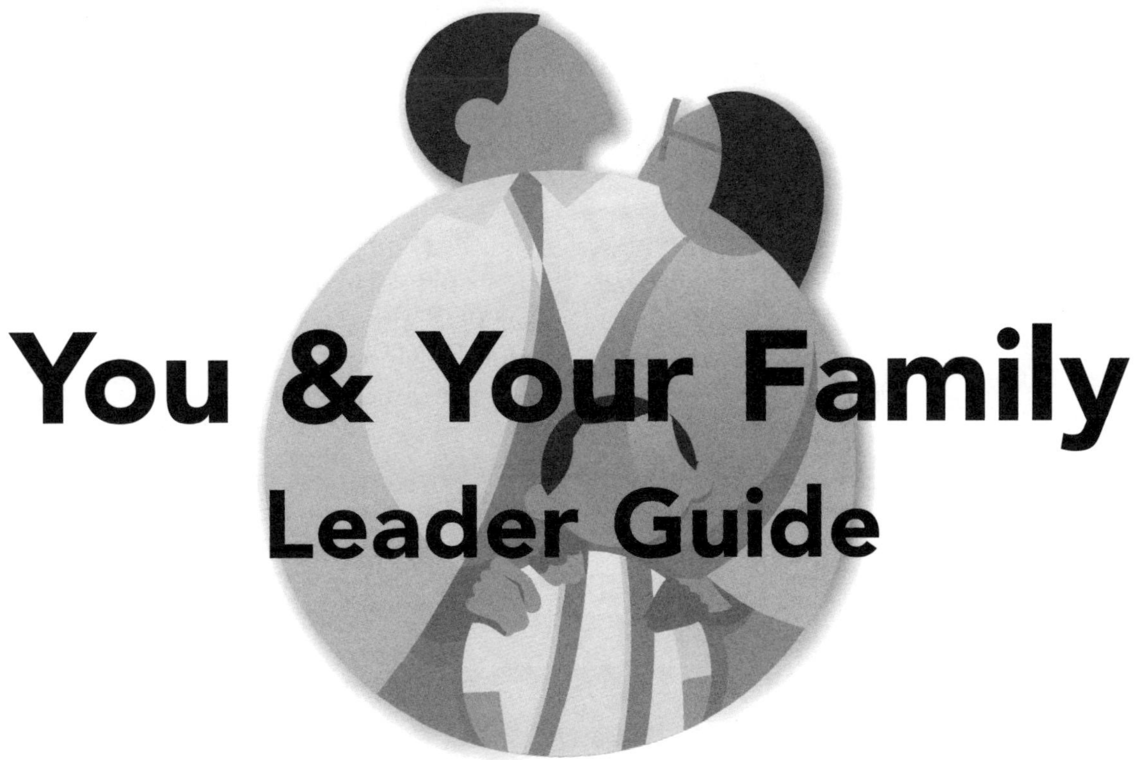

You & Your Family
Leader Guide

Aaron Morgan

**With Resource Items Adapted
From Material Written By**

**Robert Brent • Jim Rovira
Louis T. Smith • Gary Speer
Larry Thomas**

1445 Boonville Avenue
Springfield, MO 65802–1894
02–0252

Staff

National Director: Arlyn R. Pember
Editor in Chief: Michael H. Clarensau
Adult Editor: Paul W. Smith
Series Coordinator: Aaron D. Morgan
Design/Cover Illustration: Jared Van Bruaene

The book for which this leader guide is designed can be ordered from Gospel Publishing House (02–0152) at 1–800–641–4310.

The Biblical Living Series

The *Biblical Living Series* is designed to reflect the following five principles, which are essential to the learning process. To fully implement this study material, embrace these philosophical statements and make them a part of your own philosophy of small group leadership.

1. **Christians primarily study the Bible to learn how to live for God, not to pick up trivial facts.**

   Most people in your group are not interested in learning names, dates, and other bits of data unless doing so can help them live better lives for the Lord and others. Each meeting looks at biblical passages deep enough for group members to understand the principles for Christian living those passages teach.

2. **Prior, individual study allows group meetings to focus on practical application.**

   Why take up valuable meeting time going over things that could have been learned at home? Having group members complete the book chapter prior to the meeting allows all of your time together to be used to help them apply what they have learned.

3. **Everyone's interests and learning style are different, so various methods must be used to teach them.**

   You know best what interests your group and what will help them to get the most out of the meetings. The Leader Sheets allow you to customize each meeting to fit those in your group.

4. **Honest, accountable relationships do more to change lives than fact-filled lectures.**

   One reason people join small groups and Sunday School classes is to meet their need for close relationships with other believers. Every meeting includes activities that help group members accept, listen to, and challenge each other.

5. **Leaders can impact group members the most through one-on-one interaction and prayer.**

   Relational teaching is becoming the norm, making personal contact outside the meeting essential to seeing group members live out individually what they have discussed as a group. And because no one can live for God consistently without the aid of His Spirit, prayer is your most effective "contact" with group members.

You & Your Family

Knowing how others handle family relationships helps us improve our own.

Materials

- copies of the book *You & Your Family*
- photocopies of Resources A and B

Suggested Prayer

"We are grateful, God, that You have called us to a relationship with You and included us in Your family. We also desire to have good relationships with our human families, to foster love and respect. Stir in us an even greater desire to have close, God-centered, family relationships."

Inspect

☑ Discussion

Give each group member a copy of *You & Your Family*. Highlight the book's back cover and contents page, letting every person answer the question: "Which part of this book do you anticipate will be most helpful to you? Why is that so?"

Reflect

☑ Work Sheet: "What Is A Family?"

Hand out copies of Resource A. Have the group members complete them individually before discussing their answers as a group.

Connect

☑ Work Sheet: "My Family's Spiritual History"

Distribute copies of Resource B. Have the group members fill it in as completely as possible during the group meeting. Encourage them to find out the remaining information and add it during the week.

New Needs

- ____
- ____
- ____
- ____

What Is A Family?

There are almost as many approaches to being a family as there are families. The box below contains 30 synonyms for a group of people. Circle five synonyms that describe, at least in part, what you believe a family ought to be. Then write the words in the blanks below the box and explain what about those words is like a good family.

Alliance	Club	Crowd	Gang	Platoon
Body	Coalition	Democracy	League	Posse
Bunch	Colony	Dictatorship	Network	Society
Cast	Community	Ensemble	Orchestra	Team
Clan	Company	Flock	Pack	Tribe
Clique	Crew	Fraternity	Party	Troop

______________________:

______________________:

______________________:

______________________:

______________________:

My Family's Spiritual History

Maternal GrandFather

____
Name

❏ Unsaved   ❏ Saved: _________
Age/Year

Denomination: _______________

Paternal GrandMother

____
Name

❏ Unsaved   ❏ Saved: _________
Age/Year

Denomination: _______________

Maternal GrandMother

____
Name

❏ Unsaved   ❏ Saved: _________
Age/Year

Denomination: _______________

Paternal GrandFather

____
Name

❏ Unsaved   ❏ Saved: _________
Age/Year

Denomination: _______________

Mother

____
Name

❏ Unsaved   ❏ Saved: _________
Age/Year

Denomination: _______________

Father

____
Name

❏ Unsaved   ❏ Saved: _________
Age/Year

Denomination: _______________

Learning From Your Parents

Parental influence has a continuing impact on the life of an adult.

Materials

- photocopies of Resources 1A and 1B
- 1˝ x 9˝ strips of yellow construction paper, felt-tip markers, and glue sticks
- sheets of lined paper

Suggested Prayer

"We call on You, Lord, as our perfect Heavenly Father, to help us to honor our earthly parents. We respect their experience and the efforts they have made to raise us well. Lead us in discovering ways to return to our parents the love and care they have given to us."

Inspect

❏ Discussion: Book Question 1–4

"Did the Israelites continue to honor their parents through the following generations? What was the result? Is there a parallel to today's society?"

❏ Activity: Parent Necklace

Have a student read Proverbs 1:8,9 aloud while giving each group member 20 paper strips, a marker, and a glue stick. Have them write one thing they have learned from their parents on each of their paper strips. Then have them bend one strip into a circle with the writing on the outside and glue the ends together. Have them continue to glue their strips into rings, making sure that each ring links with the previous one. The twentieth ring must link both ends of the chain, creating a necklace. As the group members are completing this activity, discuss with them that its purpose is not to do a child's craft, but to help them remember all they have learned from their parents.

Reflect

❏ Discussion: Book Question 1–6

"Does God expect you to honor your parents even if they are ungodly or do not seem worthy of respect? Explain your answer."

❏ Discussion: Book Question 1–8

"What, in your opinion, must be the main priority for believers who truly honor their parents when making decisions about providing care?"

❑ **Work Sheet: "Thoughts On Parents And Parenting"**

Divide the group into four subgroups and hand out copies of Resource 1A. Assign one question to each of the subgroups and give them 5 minutes to discuss it. Then call for one person from each subgroup to summarize his or her subgroup's comments.

Connect

❑ Discussion: Book Question 1–3

"How good were you as a child at honoring your parents? Explain how well or poorly you honor them now that you are an adult."

❑ Discussion: Book Question 1–9

"Does asking for your parents' advice mean you must always do what they advise? How can you make sure your parents know you honor them even when you do not follow their advice?"

❑ Work Sheet: "Your Parental Relationship"

Distribute copies of Resource 1B and have the group members fill them out individually.

❑ Activity: Thank-You Letter

Hand out sheets of lined paper. Give the group members a full 10 minutes to start writing letters to their parents thanking them for all the positive contributions their mothers and fathers made in their lives. Encourage everyone to finish his or her letter at home and send it this week.

Past Needs

- ____
- ____
- ____
- ____

New Needs

- ____
- ____
- ____
- ____

Thoughts On Parents And Parenting

With your subgroup, discuss the question you were assigned. Have one person record your comments. Select another person to share these comments with the rest of the group.

A. In what ways do parents influence the family?

B. What makes parental influence so powerful and enduring?

C. What are some difficult areas of the parent/child relationship?

D. What are the most rewarding areas of the parent/child relationship?

Your Parental Relationship

1. Do you feel your parents had a positive or a negative effect on your life? Why?

2. Do you think this has affected your relationship with them now? In what way?

3. If it was a negative influence, what do you feel can be done to correct it?

4. Do you believe you are honoring your parents? If not, what can you do differently?

5. What can you learn from your parents that might be of help to you at this stage in your life?

Valuing Your Grandparents' Legacy

Grandparents can be a valuable source of counsel and spiritual example.

Materials

- photocopies of Resources 2A and 2B
- sheets of lined paper
- a list of homebound or lonely senior citizens in your church

Suggested Prayer

"God, we realize that the time we have to spend with our grandparents is limited. We desire to gain all we can from their lifetime of experiences and insights. Help us to value and accept the spiritual legacy which our grandparents will turn over to us."

Inspect

❏ Discussion: Book Question 2–5

"Why do you think respect for your elders and reverence for God are included in one command (Leviticus 19;32)? What are the implications of your answer?"

❏ Work Sheet: "Biblical Grandparents"

Distribute copies of Resource 2A. Give the group members 7 minutes to fill them out before asking the entire group to discuss the question at the bottom.

Reflect

❏ Discussion: Book Question 2–6

"How have you benefited from your grandparents' advice? Do you think respect is a fair exchange for getting to learn from their experience?"

❏ Discussion: Book Question 2–10

"How have you seen your grandparents' influence in your Christian walk?"

❏ Work Sheet: "What Is A Grandparent?"

Hand out copies of Resource 2B. Give the group members 5 minutes to complete them individually. Then discuss those descriptions that were commonly chosen.

Connect

❏ Discussion: Book Question 2–3

"What practical things can you do to help your grandparents as they grow older and less able to do things on their own?"

❑ **Discussion: Book Question 2–9**

"How can your grandparents help you learn more about your family history, especially its religious history?"

❑ **Activity: Interview Questions**

Distribute sheets of lined paper. Have every group member write five questions to ask each of his or her grandparents. The questions may be different or the same for every grandparent. Urge everyone to use the questions to do an informal interview of his or her grandparents in order to learn more about his or her family's spiritual heritage.

❑ **Activity: Adopt-A-Grandparent**

Prior to the group meeting, collect the names, phone numbers, addresses, and interests of homebound or lonely senior citizens in the church who could use the companionship and help of a younger adult. (Consult your pastor or church secretary before contacting the potential "grandparents.") Near the end of the group meeting, present the list and have group members choose people they would like to adopt for whatever time period you and the pastor have decided—3 months, 6 months, 1 year.

Past Needs

- ____
- ____
- ____
- ____

New Needs

- ____
- ____
- ____
- ____

Biblical Grandparents

For each grandparent mentioned in the Bible, rate your impression of the influence he or she had on his or her grandchildren. Then fill in the appropriate circles to indicate whether the grandchildren of the passages were godly or wicked.

	Grandparent's Influence Godly Evil	**Grandchild** Godly Wicked
Jacob *Genesis 48:1–6,11–16*	●━━━━━━━━●	○ ○
Joseph *Genesis 50:22,23*	●━━━━━━━━●	○ ○
Naomi *Ruth 4:13–17*	●━━━━━━━━●	○ ○
Maacah *1 Kings 15:9–13*	●━━━━━━━━●	○ ○
Athaliah *2 Kings 11:1–3,*	●━━━━━━━━●	○ ○
Lois *2 Timothy 1:5*	●━━━━━━━━●	○ ○

Is there a pattern in the relationship between a grandparent's influence and the character of the grandchild? Why do you think there is or is not a pattern?

What Is A Grandparent?

Circle all the descriptive words and phrases that reflect what you think a grandparent is (not what you think a grandparent should be). Do not pause to consider each item. At the end, write in your own descriptive words and phrases.

Accepts of new ideas	**Old**
Bull-headed	**Opinionated**
Communicates well	**Pushy**
Contemporary	**Pushover**
Cooperative	**Relates to other generations**
Distant	**Senior citizen**
Does things one way	**Smothering**
Emphasizes "good ol' days"	**Stingy**
Excited about the present	**Understanding**
Experienced	**Wise**
Generous	**Worn out**
Knows how to give and take	_______________________
Lives in the past	_______________________
Loving	_______________________
Mature	_______________________

Getting Along With Your Siblings

God places great importance on positive sibling relationships.

Materials

- photocopies of Resources 3A and 3B
- sheets of lined paper

Suggested Prayer

"Jesus, You are a faithful Brother. We want to treat our siblings with the selfless kindness You have shown to us. Guide us in using wisdom and love to overcome any differences between us so that we can help each other live for You."

Inspect

❏ Discussion

"Name a set of siblings mentioned in the Bible. What about their relationship is exemplary? What should be avoided in your relationships with your siblings?"

❏ Activity: Creative Writing

Hand out sheets of lined paper. Have everyone imagine he or she is a servant in the household of Isaac and Rebekah on the day Jacob took Esau's blessing. Then have each group member write a one-page essay from the point of view of this imaginary servant. Whose side, if any, is he or she on? What other events might have led up to this event? If asked by Isaac or Rebekah, what would he or she suggest as a solution to the split between Jacob and Esau? What might he or she say to one of the twins to help him make peace between them?

Reflect

❏ Discussion: Book Question 3–3

"What faults do you thinks your siblings would say you have?"

❏ Discussion: Book Question 3–5

"How do you and your siblings' priorities differ? What can you learn from the things your siblings consider important?"

❏ Work Sheet: "Sibling Rivalry"

Divide the group into subgroups of three or four. Distribute copies of Resource 3A. Have the subgroups come up with their own "Top 10" list based on personal experiences and observations. After 7 minutes, regather the group and allow the subgroups to share their top three reasons for sibling rivalry.

Connect

❏ **Discussion: Book Question 3–7**

"How could you take the first step in solving a disagreement between you and a sibling?"

❏ **Discussion: Book Question 3–10**

"What have you been holding against a sibling that you need to forgive him or her for even if he or she does not make the first move?"

❏ **Work Sheet: "Individuality And Sibling Harmony"**

Distribute copies of Resource 3B. Have the group members complete them individually before discussing as a group their answers to the third and fourth questions.

❏ **Activity: Speaking For Your Sibling**

Divide the group into pairs. Have one person in each pairing share—from the point of view of the sibling with which he or she has the least in common—what it was like to be raised in his or her family. Encourage the group members to be as honest and accurate as possible in sharing their siblings' perspectives. The listening partners can ask questions to encourage the others to share openly. After 4 minutes, have the pairs reverse roles. Then regather the group and discuss briefly how trying to place oneself in a sibling's shoes helps one to better understand and accept him or her.

Past Needs

- ____
- ____
- ____
- ____

New Needs

- ____
- ____
- ____
- ____

Sibling Rivalry

List in order of importance what you feel are the 10 most important reasons many brothers and sisters experience difficulty in getting along.

1.

2.

3.

4.

5.

6.

7.

8.

9.

10.

Individuality And Sibling Harmony

1. In what ways did your family encourage or discourage individuality?

2. What effect has your family's approach to individuality had on the relationships between you and your siblings as adults?

3. If you are, or will be, a parent, what can you do to encourage your children's individuality?

4. What else could you do to promote harmony between your children?

Improving Your Relative Relationships

God can help you with extended family relationships.

Materials

- photocopies of Resources 4A and 4B

Suggested Prayer

"Lord, we want to take the fullest advantage possible of the extended family you have given us. We ask that you help our relationships with these relatives to be close, godly, and characterized by mutual love and servanthood."

Inspect

❏ Discussion: Book Question 4–6

"Read 2 Kings 11:2. How does Jehosheba's saving Joash illustrate a devoted relationship between an aunt and a nephew?"

❏ Work Sheet: "Relative Traits"

Distribute copies of Resource 4A and have the group members fill them out individually.

Reflect

❏ Discussion: Book Question 4–3

"How much would you sacrifice to help one of your cousins or your entire extended family? What does your answer indicate about the value you place on these relationships?"

❏ Discussion: Book Question 4–11

"What have you learned from the unique perspective and advice of your in-laws?"

❏ Role Play: In-Law Theatre Presents...

Call for two pairs of volunteers, with a man and a woman in each pair. Have each pair give a 2-minute role play in which they are a husband and a wife discussing one or more in-laws. The first pair should reinforce society's stereotypes of in-law relationships. The second pair is to talk about an in-law in a respectful, God-pleasing manner. After the role plays have been presented, discuss the differences between the two with the entire group.

Connect

❏ Discussion: Book Question 4–2

"What things have distanced you from your cousins? If you have grown apart, how could you renew a closer relationship?"

❏ **Discussion: Book Question 4–8**

"Select one aunt or uncle you would like to know better. What can you do this month to foster a closer relationship?"

❏ **Work Sheet: "How Do You Relate?"**

Divide the group into subgroups of two or three and distribute copies of Resource 4B. Have the subgroups discuss the questions among themselves, writing theirs and each other's answers in the spaces provided.

❏ **Activity: Praying For Unsaved Relatives**

Explain to the group that a believer in good relationship with his or her unsaved relatives will balance loving acceptance with the desire to see them saved. Then divide the group into pairs. Give the pairs 5 minutes to share with each other about their unsaved relatives. Then have them spend the next 5 minutes praying they will be sensitive to the Holy Spirit in witnessing to their unbelieving relatives and that these relatives will accept Christ.

Past Needs

- ____
- ____
- ____
- ____

New Needs

- ____
- ____
- ____
- ____

Relative Traits

This chapter's Bible passages use relationships between extended family members to illustrate several contrasting pairs of interpersonal traits. In the space below each pair of relatives, write how that pair illustrates the trait listed above it.

Opportunism   vs.   Selflessness

Joseph and the Ishmaelites   *Esther and Mordecai*

Deception   vs.   Devotion

Jacob and Laban   *Jehosheba and Joash*

Paul and his nephew

Subterfuge   vs.   Wise Council

Saul and David   *Jethro and Moses*

How Do You Relate?

1. Have you ever put yourself first at the expense of the needs of a relative? What happened?

Person A   **Person B**   **Person C**

2. How have you been blessed by the selfless love of someone in your family?

Person A   **Person B**   **Person C**

3. How has honest communication contributed positively to your family relationships?

Person A   **Person B**   **Person C**

4. How have you displayed family loyalty to your relatives?

Person A   **Person B**   **Person C**

5. What adjustments have you had to make to get along with your in-laws?

Person A   **Person B**   **Person C**

6. How might you relate differently to younger relatives as you get older?

Person A   **Person B**   **Person C**

Learning God's Marriage Design

The Bible reveals what God desires for married couples.

Materials

- photocopies of Resources 5A and 5B
- two different colored lumps of play dough or modeling clay
- blank index cards

Suggested Prayer

"Our desire, God, is that our marriages be, not what we think they need to be, but what You designed them to be. Help us to learn today the kind of marriage relationship You want us to have, then give us the will and strength to live out that ideal."

Inspect

❑ Discussion: Book Question 5–6

"Explain the reasoning Jesus used to declare that marriage should not be ended except through death (Matthew 19:3–6)."

❑ Work Sheet: "Principles For A Godly Marriage"

Distribute copies of Resource 5A and have the group members fill them out individually or as couples (if their spouses are present).

Reflect

❑ Discussion: Book Question 5–3

"If oneness is the purpose of marriage, why do you think the vast majority of married couples do not seem to experience it?"

❑ Discussion: Book Question 5–7

"What justifications have you heard others make concerning their divorces? How do these measure up to God's idea of marriage's permanence?"

❑ Activity: Illustration In Clay

Hold up two different colored lumps of play dough or modeling clay, explaining that they represent a husband and a wife. Knead the lumps together into a new, larger lump so that the colors are mingled well but still distinct. Point out that while the husband and wife are still discernable, they are also one. Have a group member try to separate the two colors of dough or clay. Then allow him or her to explain how the difficulty of separating the two illustrates the oneness of the marriage relationship.

Connect

❑ Discussion: Book Question 5–5

"What can you do this week to help there be more unity and less individualism between you and your spouse?"

❑ Discussion: Book Question 5–12

"About which aspect of God's marriage design have you been more influenced by current trends and views? What can you do this month to help your marriage be more like God desires?"

❑ Work Sheet: "Holy Matrimony?"

Distribute copies of Resource 5B and have the group members answer the questions and determine what areas they will target for improvement in the near future. If most of the group members have their spouses present, have the couples review each other's work sheets to encourage honesty and accountability.

❑ Activity: Appreciation Of Consideration

Give each group member an index card, and have him or her write some of the considerate acts his or her spouse has done and why these acts meant so much to him or her. Then have everyone record three ideas for showing consideration in return. Instruct them to use these cards as bookmarks in their Bibles to remind them to pray about their marriages during their devotional times.

Past Needs

- ____
- ____
- ____
- ____

New Needs

- ____
- ____
- ____
- ____

Principles For A Godly Marriage

Examine the following principles from Genesis 2:24 and suggest ways they have been or can be applied to your marriage.

Severance

"A man will leave his father and mother..."

List the ways you have already left your parents—literally and figuratively—since you married.

In what ways can you further apply this principle in your marriage?

Permanence

"...and be united to his wife,..."

The word translated "be united" is a strong word meaning "to glue" or "to cling." How have you already clung to your spouse?

In what ways can you strengthen your marriage by clinging to or being glued to your spouse?

Unity

"...and they will become one flesh."

Unity involves more than physical intimacy. List other ways in which unity is achieved in a marriage.

How can these ideas be put into practice in your marriage?

Holy Matrimony?

Many Christian couples do not recognize or foster the unique close relationship they can have with each other as fellow believers. Use the following questions to test the spiritual level of your marriage. Then describe the areas of your marriage's spirituality in which you will make improvements.

1. Do you thank God daily for your spouse? If so, what do you often thank Him for?

2. Do you pray daily for your spouse? If so, what do you usually pray for?

3. Do you pray daily with your spouse? If so, what do your regularly pray about?

4. Do you study the Bible daily with your spouse? If so, how do you help each other learn from it?

5. What else are you doing to help your spouse grow in spiritual maturity?

6. What do you admire about your spouse's character?

7. What do you admire about your spouse's relationship with God?

Areas To Improve This Week:

Building A Solid Relationship

With effort and God's help, a strong marriage can be built.

Materials

- photocopies of Resources 6A and 6B
- sheets of lined paper

Suggested Prayer

"Father, we recognize that no marriage is built overnight or without effort. We commit ourselves now to putting in the right effort in the right areas to build a marriage that is well-grounded and stable. And if we have laid a faulty foundation in the past, help us to repair what is wrong and replace it with traits and attitudes that are right."

Inspect

❏ Discussion

"How are the instructions in Ephesians 5:21–33 to husbands and wives really two sides of the same coin, so to speak?"

❏ Activity: Creative Writing

Hand out sheets of lined paper before reading Genesis 2:21–25 to the group. When you are finished reading, have the group members rewrite the passage in first person from a unique perspective. This might be from the viewpoint of a child reciting the story in Sunday School, of Adam telling his teenage sons what happened, of Eve remembering the event, of one of the angels who might have seen what happened, or even of God himself. The only rule is that story must explain what it might mean to be "one flesh."

Reflect

❏ Discussion: Book Question 6–3

"What is the danger of thinking that sexual fulfillment alone is enough to keep you faithful? What else is required?"

❏ Discussion: Book Question 6–5

"What have you given up in order to better serve your spouse? How has this been a rewarding experience?"

❏ Activity: "The Voice Of Experience"

Prior to the group meeting, select three mature couples to form a panel. Give each couple a copy of Resource 6A and review it with them so that they understand all the questions ahead of time and can be thinking of how to answer them.

During the group meeting, have the panel sit before the group while you have them answer selected questions from Resource 6A. Encourage them to be brief, yet candid. While the aim of this activity is not to embarrass anyone, tactful honesty will best help the group members learn from the the panelists' experiences. (You may want to make this activity double or triple length to allow for more questions and group interaction.)

Connect

❏ Discussion: Book Question 6–8

"Have you unrealistically expected your spouse to meet all your needs? What needs and desires can you turn over to the Lord and allow Him to answer?"

❏ Discussion: Book Question 6–12

"What can you do this week to improve the intimacy between you and your spouse?"

❏ Work Sheet: "Getting To Know You"

Distribute copies of Resource 6B and have the group members complete them individually.

❏ Activity: Gender Perspectives

Divide the group by gender and have the men and women gather separately to discuss the issue of mutual sacrifice from their unique perspectives. Make sure there is a mature leader in each subgroup to guide the discussion. Have the men share their failures and successes in leading with sensitivity. Have the women discuss the pitfalls and rewards of learning how to trust and find security in their very human husbands.

After 7 minutes, bring the men and women together and hand out slips of paper to the entire group. Based on what they learned in their discussions, have the group members write an attitude or action they will work on this week that will help them better sacrifice for the good of their spouses.

Past Needs

- ____
- ____
- ____
- ____

New Needs

- ____
- ____
- ____
- ____

The Voice Of Experience

Select the questions below that you think would best help your group members in their own marriages and ask them of the three-couple panel you have chosen.

Committing To Be Faithful

Where have you, as individuals and couples, found the balance between paranoia and permissiveness? Was this determined from the beginning or discovered over time?

How have you dealt with our society's pressure to devalue your marriage commitments? What has kept you together despite the inevitable difficulties of marriage?

Learning To Sacrifice

Wives: Learning to trust someone completely is very difficult. How have you realistically learned to depend on your husband, or are you still learning?

Husbands: How have you learned to love selflessly, or are you still learning as well?

Fostering Intimacy

What discoveries have you made about yourself and your spouse in the years you have been married? How close do you feel to completely understanding your marriage?

What unreasonable expectations did each of you have about sex when you married? How did you adjust those expectations over time to bring greater closeness between you?

Getting To Know You

Whether you think it of major or little consequence, each detail about yourself that you share with your spouse helps him or her know and trust you more. Foster further intimacy in your marriage by answering the following questions and sharing those answers with your spouse. You may choose to have an official answer exchange or to casually bring up these details about yourself in conversation. Either way, this activity may be the prod you need to be more transparent with your husband or wife.

1. What is your earliest, childhood memory?

2. What smells do you remember from your home?

3. Describe your first pet or favorite stuffed animal.

4. On whom did you have your first crush? What did you like about him or her?

5. What is the first thing you remember wanting to be when you grew up? What did you want to be when you were in junior high? High school?

6. What is the most important thing you have learned from your parents?

7. Have your parents or someone else you trust ever hurt you deeply? If so, how have you handled it?

8. What is your greatest phobia? Why do you think you have it?

9. If you could change one thing about your character or personality, what would it be? Why?

10. What quirk or habit of your spouse do you love the most? Why?

Making It Last

Ongoing love and respect are essential for a fulfilling marriage.

Materials

- photocopies of Resources 7A and 7B

Suggested Prayer

"Lord, we acknowledge that a lasting, fulfilling marriage is only possible when both of us are yielded to You and have allowed Your character to shape our own. And we are determined to do all we can—with Your help—to keep our relationship vibrant and growing."

Inspect

❏ Discussion

"First Corinthians 7:32–35 seems to say that married people are not as devoted to the Lord as singles are. What do you think Paul meant in this passage?"

❏ Work Sheet: "Christlike Love For My Spouse"

Distribute copies of Resource 7A and have the group members complete them. Then lead the group in discussing how two of the verses listed could be applied to loving their spouses.

Reflect

❏ Discussion: Book Question 7–4

"Ideally, both you and your spouse will look out for each others' interests. What are you to do if your spouse does not take this responsibility seriously?"

❏ Discussion: Book Question 7–7

"How could you alert yourself if you were not submitting to—that is, showing proper respect for—your spouse?"

❏ Activity: Role Play

Have two volunteers—male and female—perform a 1-minute role play depicting how spouses can take each other for granted after several years together. Then have the group discuss how the couple demonstrated a lack of consideration, honor, and selfless love.

Connect

❏ Discussion: Book Question 7–2

"Do you find it difficult to do things for your spouse that you do not want to do? How could you improve in this area?"

❑ **Discussion: Book Question 7–5**

"What three things could you start doing this week for your spouse that would show him or her that you are concerned about his or her needs and desires?"

❑ **Work Sheet: "Do You Honor Your Spouse?"**

Distribute copies of Resource 7B. Have the group members use them to evaluate how well or poorly they honor their spouses. Then discuss the last question as a group.

❑ **Activity: Future Thinking**

Lead the group members in describing what they think their marriages will be like in 10 years, in 20 years, and in 30 years. Have everyone concentrate on the possibilities if they continue to work at keeping their marriages healthy and vibrant.

Past Needs

- ____
- ____
- ____
- ____

New Needs

- ____
- ____
- ____
- ____

Christlike Love For My Spouse

While on earth, Jesus said much about love and demonstrated it even more. For every verse or passage recorded below, write how you might apply what Jesus said or did in your marriage.

Love your enemies and pray for those who persecute you…If you love those who love you, what reward will you get? (Matthew 5:44,46).

Take my yoke upon you and learn from me, for I am gentle and humble in heart, and you will find rest for your souls (Matthew 11:29).

Jesus replied: " 'Love the Lord your God with all your heart and with all your soul and with all your mind.' This is the first and greatest commandment. And the second is like it: 'Love your neighbor as yourself.' All the Law and the Prophets hang on these two commandments" (Matthew 22:37–40).

It was just before the Passover Feast. Jesus knew that the time had come for him to leave this world and go to the Father. Having loved his own who were in the world, he now showed them the full extent of his love (John 13:1).

My command is this: Love each other as I have loved you. Greater love has no one than this, that he lay down his life for his friends (John 15:12,13).

Do You Honor Your Spouse?

Read the following dictionary definitions of honor before answering the questions below:

Honor *n* [ME, fr. OF *honor*, fr. L *honos*, *honor*] (13c) **1 a :** good name or public esteem : REPUTATION **b :** a showing of usu. merited respect : RECOGNITION ⟨pay ~ to our founder⟩ **8 a :** a keen sense of ethical conduct : INTEGRITY **b :** one's word given as a guarantee of performance

syn HONOR, HOMAGE, REVERENCE, DEFERENCE mean respect and esteem shown to another. HONOR may apply to the recognition of one's right to great respect or to any expression of such recognition. HOMAGE adds the implication of accompanying praise. REVERENCE implies profound respect mingled with love, devotion, or awe. DEFERENCE implies yielding or submitting to another's judgment or preference out of respect or reverence. *syn* see in addition HONESTY.

Honor *vt* **hon•ored; hon•or•ing** (13c) **1 a :** to regard or treat with honor or respect **b :** to confer honor on **2 a :** to live up to or fulfill the terms of ⟨~ a commitment⟩

1. Having a fuller understanding of the word *honor*, would you say that you truly honor your spouse? Explain your answer.

2. What makes your spouse someone worthy of "merited respect"?

3. What do you think of the idea of giving or showing your spouse homage, reverence, and deference?

4. How have you demonstrated integrity by fulfilling your wedding vow to love and cherish your spouse?

5. What can you do to help yourself honor your husband or wife more?

Living Unequally Yoked

The Lord strengthens and encourages those with unsaved spouses.

Materials

- photocopies of Resources 8A and 8B
- sheets of lined paper

Suggested Prayer

"None of us, Lord, wants a marriage that is anything less than Your ideal. We know this means that both of us must have You as Lord. Those of us who have an unsaved spouse ask You to help us live for You in such a way that our husband or wife is drawn to You. And those of us who are not yet married or have a believing spouse pledge to discourage believers from marrying unbelievers while maintaining compassionate empathy for those who are already in such marriages."

Inspect

❑ **Discussion: Book Question 8–2**

"What do you think it means to be 'yoked together' (2 Corinthians 6:14)?"

❑ **Work Sheet: "Unholy Alliances: 2 Corinthians 6:14–16"**

Distribute copies of Resource 8A. Then divide the group into subgroups of three or four and have these subgroups read the formatted Bible passage and answer the four questions together. You may want to review one or two of the questions with the entire group.

Reflect

❑ **Discussion: Book Question 8–7**

"If your spouse does not turn to the Lord despite your best efforts, what can you do to be spiritually and emotionally fulfilled?"

❑ **Discussion: Book Question 8–10**

"What role do you think prayer can play in a marriage between a believer and a non-Christian, both for the praying spouse and for the one being prayed for?"

❑ **Case Study: "Slippery Slope"**

Distribute copies of Resource 8B. Read the case study to the group before having them answer the questions that follow. Encourage them make sure these answers are not simplistic, but realistically take into account the emotions of those involved.

Connect

❏ Discussion: Book Question 8–8

"What can you do to help yourself pursue your relationship with God without making your unsaved spouse feel shut out of that area of your life?"

❏ Discussion: Book Question 8–11

"Think of a Christian friend or family member who is in a relationship with an unsaved person. From the principles discussed in this meeting, what could you share with him or her that might make a difference?"

❏ Activity: Letter Writing

Hand out sheets of lined paper and have the group members draft letters. If a person is writing to his or her own unsaved spouse, encourage him or her to express an equal mix of loving acceptance, affirmation of what is good in the marriage, and gentle notice that he or she will continue to live for the Lord and pray for his or her spouses' salvation. If writing to a Christian friend who is married to or dating an unbeliever, urge group members to offer empathy and encouragement rather than advice.

❏ Activity: Prayer For Unsaved Spouses

Have the group members pray individually for the salvation of husbands and wives, either their own or a fellow believer's, who are unsaved. Also have group members gather around any who are trying to live successfully with an unsaved spouse and pray that God will give these believers strength, peace, and joy in this difficult situation.

Past Needs

- ____
- ____
- ____
- ____

New Needs

- ____
- ____
- ____
- ____

Unholy Alliances: 2 Corinthians 6:14–16

Do not be **yoked together** with [*Believers,*] *unbelievers.*

For what do have **in common**? *righteousness* and *wickedness*

Or what **fellowship** can *light* have with *darkness?*

What **harmony** is there between *Christ* and *Belial?*

What does have **in common** with a ***believer*** an *unbeliever?*

What **agreement** is there between the ***temple of God*** and *idols?*

1. What various kinds of relationships are described by phrases such as "yoked together with," "in common with," "fellowship…with," "harmony between," and "agreement between"?

2. This passage repeatedly asks "what" good and evil have in common, with the implied answer "nothing!" How might recognizing this sharp contrast help a believer understand how serious the differences between him or her and an unbelieving person are?

3. This passage assumes believers are observably different from unbelievers in character, world view, and motivation. What about believers who only serve the Lord halfheartedly? Do they need to heed this passage or can they ignore it?

4. How do you think a Christian can balance the need to witness relationally to unbelievers against the dangers of being spiritually compromised by close relationships with them?

Slippery Slope

Suzanne Mendolson was a Christian. She lived in a sparsely populated rural community and attended a small church. Like many single young adults, Suzanne desired to marry and raise a family. There was, however, a problem: the pickings were quite slim—non-existent, in fact, as far as she could tell. All the Christian men her age were either married or engaged. As time passed, Suzanne grew increasingly depressed about the prospect of remaining single.

The store where Suzanne worked got a new employee. Joash was well-mannered and thoughtful. A relationship started to develop between them. They began spending a lot of time together after hours. Joash even attended Sunday services periodically with Suzanne, claiming he was a Christian and that he believed in God.

As time passed, Suzanne and Joash continued to grow closer. Eventually, he proposed, she accepted, and they were married. Suzanne was certain things could not have been better. Or so she thought.

Within a year Joash stopped going to church altogether and even started giving Suzanne a hard time about attending so much herself. More arguments came later when the couple had children and Suzanne began taking them with her on Sunday mornings. The constant struggle over church wore her down, until her commitment to the Lord had been weakened. Despite her good intentions, Suzanne stopped taking the children to church and found it very hard to make any spiritual progress.

1. Where do you think Suzanne went wrong in her relationship with Joash?

2. What could Suzanne have done differently?

3. How would you advise Suzanne to handle John's protests about her and the children's church attendance?

Overcoming Adultery

God's mercy restores lives broken by adulterous relationships.

Materials

- photocopies of Resources 9A and 9B
- a television, video cassette player, and a Christian instructional video about adultery

Suggested Prayer

"Father, we understand that marriage is, in many ways, a reflection of the relationship we can have with You. And so we understand that each of us is to show his or her spouse the unconditional love and faithfulness You have demonstrated to us. Let there be both purity and forgiveness in our marriages."

Inspect

❏ Discussion: Book Question 9–12

"Read Psalm 51. How important is it that David recognized both his wickedness and his unworthiness to be forgiven?"

❏ Work Sheet: "Biblical Principles About Adultery"

Distribute copies of Resource 9A and have the group members complete it individually. If there is time, have everyone compare the matches they made. (The following list of letters in their suggested matched order is given with the understanding that some passages could be summarized by several principles: I, H, J, B, F, D/J, E, A, G, C.)

Reflect

❏ Discussion: Book Question 9–5

"Have you seen others fall into adultery making 'minor mistakes'? How did things progress to sexual immorality?"

❏ Discussion: Book Question 9–7

"Is there a difference between the natural consequences of a sin and God's judgment? Why or why not?"

❏ Activity: Video Segment

Play about 5 minutes of a Christian instructional video dealing with either the prevention of or restoration after adultery. (Preferably, the video should bring out points not discussed or addressed in *You & Your Family*.) Then lead the group in discussing what they watched.

Connect

❏ **Discussion: Book Question 9–4**

"What two things can you do this week to revitalize your relationships with God and your spouse?"

❏ **Discussion: Book Question 9–14**

"What have you learned from this chapter that will most help you affair-proof your marriage?"

❏ **Work Sheet: "Praying Psalm 51"**

Distribute copies of Resource 9B. Have the group members write their own paraphrases of David's prayer as a pattern of true repentance.

❏ **Activity: Counseling Referral**

Have a local Christian counselor or psychologist share with the group what a professional counselor can do to help them develop and maintain healthy marriages, handle tempting situations, end an affair, or find forgiveness for and rebuild a marriage after adultery has been committed.

Past Needs

- ____
- ____
- ____
- ____

New Needs

- ____
- ____
- ____
- ____

Biblical Principles About Adultery

Match the following principles about adultery with the Bible verses and passages below.

A. Adultery is an attitude as well as an action.

B. Adulterers deserve extreme and immediate punishment.

C. Adultery is a sin against the One who created you and lives in you.

D. Adultery damages both the adulterer and the spouse who remained faithful.

E. Adulterers try to deny feelings of guilt.

F. Adultery is much less tempting for those who enjoy and appreciate their spouses.

G. Even the godly must guard against adultery.

H. Adultery reveals and worsens corrupt character.

I. God forbids adultery of any degree.

J. Adultery is almost always accompanied by deception and shame.

_____ You shall not commit adultery (Exodus 20:14).

_____ Do not have sexual relations with your neighbor's wife and defile yourself with her (Leviticus 18:20).

_____ The eye of the adulterer watches for dusk; he thinks, "No eye will see me," and he keeps his face concealed (Job 24:15).

_____ If a man is found sleeping with another man's wife, both the man who slept with her and the woman must die. You must purge the evil from Israel (Deuteronomy 22:22).

_____ Rejoice in the wife of your youth. A loving doe, a graceful dear—may her breasts satisfy you always, may you ever be captivated by her love (Proverbs 5:18,19).

_____ A man who commits adultery lacks judgment; whoever does so destroys himself. Blows and disgrace are his lot, and his shame will never be wiped away (Proverbs 6:32,33).

_____ An adulteress…eats and wipes her mouth and says, 'I've done nothing wrong" (Proverbs 30:20).

_____ You have heard that it was said, "Do not commit adultery." But I tell you that anyone who looks at a woman lustfully has already committed adultery with her in his heart (Matthew 5:27,28).

_____ You who say that people should not commit adultery, do you commit adultery? (Romans 2:22).

_____ He who sins sexually sins against his own body. Do you not know that your body is a temple of the Holy Spirit?…Therefore honor God with your body (1 Corinthians 6:18).

Praying Psalm 51

Read each verse and the summary next to it before writing your own prayer based on that verse.

Verse 1

Have mercy on me, O God, according to your unfailing love; according to your great compassion blot out my transgressions.

Summary

David based his appeal for forgiveness on God's character, not his own worthiness.

Your Prayer

Verse 3

I know my transgressions, and my sin is always before me.

Summary

David took responsibility for his actions.

Your Prayer

Verse 4

Against you, you only, have I sinned…so that you are proved right when you speak and justified when you judge.

Summary

David acknowledged that God is perfectly justified when He condemns sin.

Your Prayer

Verse 5

Surely I was sinful at birth, sinful from the time my mother conceived me.

Summary

David recognized his fallen human nature.

Your Prayer

Verse 7

Cleanse me with hyssop, and I will be clean; wash me, and I will be whiter than snow.

Summary

David asked for the complete removal of his sin.

Your Prayer

Verse 8

Let me hear joy and gladness; let the bones you have crushed rejoice.

Summary

David desired release from his guilt.

Your Prayer

Verse 10

Create in me a pure heart, O God, and renew a steadfast spirit within me.

Summary

David depended on God to help him rebuild his character.

Your Prayer

Verse 11

Do not cast me from your presence or take your Holy Spirit from me.

Summary

David knew his unconfessed sin had almost separated him from God.

Your Prayer

You & Your Family Leader Guide

Accepting Parental Responsibilities

Godly parents raise their children according to scriptural principles.

Materials

- photocopies of Resources 10A and 10B
- sheets of lined paper

Suggested Prayer

"Heavenly Father, You are the supreme example of what a parent is to be—teacher, disciplinarian, and nurturer. Help us to be these things to our children as we develop Your characteristics in our own lives."

Inspect

❏ Discussion: Book Question 10–7

"According to 1 Samuel 2:29, Eli showed that he honored his sons more than God by not disciplining them. Is this true of all parents who do not discipline? Why or why not?"

❏ Activity: A Letter To Eli

Divide the group into pairs and hand out sheets of lined paper. Have the pairs write to Eli (the high priest of 1 Samuel whose sons were wicked). The letter can be to the elderly Eli as he appears in Scripture, giving him suggestions on how he can discipline older or adult children. Or the letter can be written to a much younger Eli when his sons were babies, explaining what he can do as a parent to see that his sons grow up disciplined. If there is enough time, reassemble the group and have everyone read each other's letters.

Reflect

❏ Discussion: Book Question 10–1

"Who was made responsible for passing God's commands to the next generation? Why do you think this was so?"

❏ Discussion: Book Question 10–9

"How does external discipline by parents transform into internal discipline—a child's self-control?"

❏ Work Sheet: "Teachable Moments"

Divide the group into pairs or triads and distribute copies of Resource 10A. Give the subgroups 1 minute to list as many day-to-day opportunities to teach children about God as possible. When the time is up, have the subgroups exchange their lists so each subgroup has a list it did not create. Give the subgroups 7 minutes to choose five of the teachable moments listed and consider how parents could take advantage of these opportunities to teach their children spiritual things.

Connect

❏ Discussion: Book Question 10–2

"What are some common situations and times in which casual discussions with your children about serving God might be started naturally?"

❏ Discussion: Book Question 10–12

"What five things could you do this week that would show your children how much you love them?"

❏ Work Sheet: "Establishing Consistent Discipline"

Hand out copies of Resource 10B. Have the group members complete them as couples (if possible) or as individuals. Even if some or all of the people in your group have no children, have them complete the work sheet anyway. It may come in handy in the future.

❏ Activity: Personal Case Studies

Divide the group into several subgroups. Give every parent an opportunity to share a current situation with his or her children for which godly counsel would be helpful. Urge everyone to give support generously and advice kindly.

Past Needs

- ____
- ____
- ____
- ____

New Needs

- ____
- ____
- ____
- ____

Teachable Moments

In 1 minute, list the spiritual teaching opportunities a parent might discover in the routine of daily living. An example as been provided to get you going.

- a Sunday School craft
-
-
-

Give this resource sheet to another subgroup.

From the list above, select five teachable moments and record below how a parent could realistically use them to teach children something about God or Christian living.

1.

2.

3.

4.

5.

Establishing Consistent Discipline

Use this work sheet as a tool in developing a consistent system of discipline for your children. Level Three, for instance, might be a 5-minute time out with several examples of misbehavior for which this level of discipline might be appropriate. For each of the levels you use, record the method of discipline and the kinds of behavior that call for that discipline. You may wish to establish a similar system of rewards for good behavior.

Level One: ___________________________

-
-
-

Level Two: ___________________________

-
-
-

Level Three: ___________________________

-
-
-

Level Four: ___________________________

-
-
-

Level Five: ___________________________

-
-
-

Leading Family Devotions

Family devotions provide a forum for teaching spiritual values.

Materials

- photocopies of both pages of Resource 11
- sheets of lined paper
- a large pad of paper and a large marker

Suggested Prayer

"God, we want our children to know who You are, what You are like, and what You want them to be like. We commit ourselves to systematically instilling spiritual knowledge and values in our children through regular family devotions tailored to the needs—spiritual, emotional, and social—of our children."

Inspect

❏ Discussion: Book Question 11–7

"How does Deuteronomy 6:8,9 affirm the need for a multi-sensory approach to teaching your children the faith?"

❏ Activity: Generation Interaction

Have a group member read Psalm 78:1–8, and have everyone skim over the rest of the psalm. Then have the group members come up with things the next generation can learn—by both positive and negative example—from the current generation of Christians. Use a thick-line marker to record their answers on a large pad of paper.

Reflect

❏ Discussion: Book Question 11–2

"How can family devotions help you to hand down your faith to your children?"

❏ Discussion: Book Question 11–10

"Why do you think it is so important that family devotions be regularly scheduled? How would you handle unavoidable time conflicts?"

❏ Activity: Devotions Role Play

Have three or four volunteers perform a role play of a family having devotions together using Proverbs 30:32,33. Give the "parents" and "children" 1 minute to prepare. Then let them role play the situation for 2 minutes. Lead the group in sharing what they would have done differently to present the passage or how they might react to the questions asked. Discuss the trial-and-error nature of successful family devotions.

Connect

❏ **Discussion: Book Question 11–4**

"In what ways would you like to see your children have a better understanding of God and His ways than you have?"

❏ **Discussion: Book Question 11–8**

"What spiritual milestones in your children's lives would you like to commemorate? What are several creative ways you might help them remember one such event?"

❏ **Information Sheet: "Family Devotion Resources"**

Distribute copies of Resource 11 and review the different kinds of family devotion resources that are available. Point out that these resources can be obtained through Gospel Publishing House (the order numbers are on the resource) or at a local Christian bookstore.

❏ **Activity: Putting A Devotion Together**

Divide the group into four subgroups and assign them various age levels—preschoolers, elementary children, teenagers, and mixed. Give each subgroup a sheet of lined paper. Have the subgroups select recorders and come up with creative and meaningful family devotion times for their assigned age-groups. The completed idea sheets can be copied and distributed at the next group meeting.

Past Needs

- ____
- ____
- ____
- ____

New Needs

- ____
- ____
- ____
- ____

Family Devotions Resources

The following materials are available through Gospel Publishing House. Catalog numbers are listed after the description of the material.

1001 Ways To Introduce Your Child To God, **by Kathy Reimer.** This book helps parents preschoolers with three questions pertaining to teaching your children—why, when, and how. (03WP2683)

Betty Lukens Felt Activity Books. Washable felt books with felt figures help children learn stories from Scripture. Each of the following books has several pages: *Bible Stories* (18WA7484), *Old Testament Bible Stories* (18WA7490), *Noah's Ark* (18WA7491), *Life Of Jesus As A Boy* (18WA7492).

Bible Books Posters. Illustrated for children, these two posters group Old and New Testament books by category. Includes a teaching guide. (08WA5980)

Bible Make-A-Story Sets. Each set has a colorful background board and 2 sheets of self-adhesive stickers that can be used repeatedly. (08WA5823, David; 08WA5824, Jesus' Birth; 08WA5825, Noah's Ark; 08WA5826, Queen Esther)

Children's Daily Devotional Bible, CEV. Every weekday's devotion encourages early readers ages 6–11 to discover the Scriptures for themselves. Also includes full-color illustrations, memory verses, interactive prayers, a Parent's Guide, People You'll Meet, and a subject index. (01WA0632, hard)

Children's Worker's Encyclopedia Of Bible Teaching Ideas. These books are packed with devotions, skits, interactive crafts, activities, prayers, field trips, service projects, music, quiet reflections, and more linked directly to specific Bible passages. Both books are indexed by verse, theme, and style. (03WA5203, Old Testament; 03WA5204, New Testament)

Crafts And More For Children's Ministry, **by Karyn Henley and Lois Keffer.** Pull kids into interactive Bible stories with a collection of 86 craft activities. The book includes everything you need, including Bible stories, directions, illustrations, and follow-up questions. (03WA3928)

Devotions For Little Boys And Girls, **by Joan C. Webb.** This book has 112 brief devotions for children ages 3–6. Each devotion includes Scripture, activity, and a prayer. (03WP1359)

Dying Of Embarrassment, **by Lorraine Peterson.** Daily devotions for teens. Includes a memory verse, application, and prayer. (03WP1380)

Every Day With God: A Child's Daily Bible. Five short Bible readings for every week cover creation to Revelation in 1 year. For children 7–10, this International Children's Bible includes daily prayers, weekly memory verses, and colorful illustrations. (03WA1434, hard)

Family Walk Devotional Bible, NIV. Geared for families with children ages 5–12, this Bible contains devotions for every weekday and weekend that are blended with the NIV text. Nineteen full-color pages answering the Big Questions children often ask are interspersed. Created by Walk Thru the Bible Ministries. (01WA0813, paper; 01WA0814, hard)

Finger Play Activities, **edited by Mary Gross.** This spiral book contains more than 200 reproducible finger play activities and games for parents of children ages 2–5. (03WA3321)

How To Lead A Child To Christ. This 15-minute video explains where to start when talking with a child, how to tell if a child understands, and when to ask a child to make a decision. (26WA0489)

How To Teach Kids Using Guided Conversation. This 15-minute video teaches you how to help a child open up and guide thinking toward biblical truths. (26WA0491)

Kids' Devotional Bible, NIrV. This full year of daily Bible readings has weekday devotions and special weekend entries. It also includes a subject guide and book introductions. (01WA0684, paper; 01WA0685, hard)

Prayer Adventures For Boys And Girls, by **Verna Nepstad.** Puzzles, comics, stories, and a prayer diary are used to help children ages 9–11 become prayer soldiers. The book explains forgiveness and the plan of salvation, defines and teaches the power of prayer, tells the importance of listening to and obeying God, gives practical ideas for finding a place and time or regular prayer, and discusses other related topics. (02WA0338, student; 02WA0348, instructor's guide)

Questions Children Ask Resources, by **David R. Veerman, James C. Galvin, James C. Wilhoit, Daryl J. Lucas, Richard Osborne, Lil Crump, Bruce B. Barton, and Jonathan Farrar.** Each of the books in this series provide biblical answers to common questions children have about various issues. The five titles are *101 Questions Children Ask About God* (03WA2166), *102 Questions Children Ask About The Bible* (03WA2166), *103 Questions Children Ask About Right From Wrong* (03WA2166), *104 Questions Children Ask About Heaven And Hell* (03WA2166), and *105 Questions Children Ask About Money Matters* (03WA2166). Every answer includes Bible verses and a cartoon illustration.

Quiet Times With God, by **Mack Thomas.** Targeting 120 foundational truths for toddlers, each theme is presented three ways, 3 days in a row, and tied together with colorful illustrations. This fun-to-read devotional also features theme verses and suggested Bible passages. (01WA0223, hard)

Tuning Up: Jammin' For Tight Relationships, by **Mark Littleton.** Eight weeks of devotions designed to help teens with relationships. Illustrated with cartoons. (03WP2727)

Written On Our Hearts, by **Susan L. Lingo.** Seven proven memory strategies, games, and activities help children have fun memorizing Scriptures. Includes information on specific learning traits of children ages 4–12. (03WA2849)

Your Family Time With God, by **John Maxwell with Brad Lewis.** Escorts a family through 52 weeks of topics with lots of suggestions for fun activities, such as making an ice cream cake, playing bean bag toss, and clipping coupons. (03WA3530)

Youthwalk Devotional Bible, NIV. Offers four-step devotions for every weekday and shorter two-step devotions for weekends. Covering more than 250 indexed topics, the devotions discuss issues teens face. The Bible is also enhanced with colorful "Hot Topic" and Bible facts pages. (01WA0318, paper; 01WA0636, hard)

Instilling Godly Character

You can help your children develop biblical character traits.

Materials

- photocopies of Resources 12A and 12B
- sheets of lined paper

Suggested Prayer

"Lord, we want our children to do more than mimic religious practices: we want them to make Your values and principles their own. We ask that You give us wisdom as we do our part in helping our children develop Christian character, attitudes, and practices."

Inspect

❏ Discussion: Book Question 12–1

"What do Matthew 12:36; 1 Corinthians 4:5; and 2 Corinthians 5:10 teach about your children's accountability to God?"

❏ Work Sheet: "Developing Godly Character"

Divide the group into two subgroups and give both of them a copy of Resource 12A. Have the subgroups read and discuss the passages assigned to them with one person in each subgroup writing things down. After 7 minutes, reassemble the group and have them share what they learned about integrity from the passages read.

Reflect

❏ Discussion: Book Question 12–4

"What traditions of respect for your elders and those in authority were you taught as a child?"

❏ Discussion: Book Question 12–6

"Jonathan was more loyal to David than to his own father. How does a person of character determine where the greater loyalty ought to be?"

❏ Activity: World Without Accountability

Pass around magazine and newspaper articles that demonstrate a refusal on one person or group's part to be accountable to another person or group. (Examples are business executives laying off workers to increase profit margins, parents not taking care of their children, or politicians reneging on campaign promises.) Discuss what the world would be like if everyone acted in this way. Then lead the discussion to the need for children to learn that they are accountable to everyone, not just those who have power over them.

Connect

❏ **Discussion: Book Question 12–12**

"What tasks can you give your children to begin teaching them to be dependable?"

❏ **Discussion: Book Question 12–13**

"What additional character traits and godly values do you hope to instill in your children?"

❏ **Case Study: "Honesty In Every Situation"**

Distribute copies of Resource 12B and have group members complete them individually. After 7 minutes, have the group discuss their choices.

❏ **Activity: Brainstorming**

Divide the group into subgroups of three to five people. Give each subgroup a sheet of lined paper and have a person write across the top line "Ways To Develop A Child's Character." For the next 5 minutes, have the subgroups brainstorm about methods of passing on godly values to children. These can be untried ideas or tested practices. Regather the group and review all the suggestions. (It may be helpful to collect the sheets and have them compiled into a single, typed page which can be copied and distributed at the next group meeting—if this is an ongoing group—or mailed to those present.)

Past Needs

- ____
- ____
- ____
- ____

New Needs

- ____
- ____
- ____
- ____

Developing Godly Character

Group 1

Read Philippians 4:8,9 and Ephesians 5:1,2 and 6:10–17. In the space below, describe how these passages instruct believers to develop godly character.

Group 2

Read Colossians 3:5–17 and 1 Timothy 6:11. In the space below, describe how these passages instruct believers to develop godly character.

Honesty In Every Situation

One of your children decided to set up a lemonade stand. He or she made a large, cheerful sign to hang in front of the stand: "Fresh Squeezed Lemonade." Together, you bought a large bag of lemons at the store and juiced them. Just as the day got hot, you and your child set the stand up and start selling the lemonade you had made from scratch.

Business was better than expected: by early in the afternoon, all the lemonade was gone. While your child ate lunch inside, you ran to the store for more lemons. But when you got there, you decided to buy frozen concentrate lemonade to save time. When you got home, you opened the cans and started making more lemonade, only to have your child stop you and say: "We can't use that stuff! The sign outside says 'fresh squeezed.'"

What do you do? Circle an option below and explain why you chose it.

A. Ignore him or her.

B. Explain that your customers will not know the difference

C. Go back to the store for real lemons.

D. Suggest that you and your child make a new sign.

You took one of your children with you to the mall to buy a birthday gift for your spouse. You found the perfect gift and took it to the purchase counter. The salesperson asked you the price because the tag was missing. Your child blurted out a price that was a little less than what you remembered it being.

What do you do? Circle an option below and explain why you chose it.

A. Give the correct price and find out later why your child stated the price he or she did.

B. Pretend the price your child stated is correct.

C. Ignore him or her and go back to see what exactly the price is.

D. Assume your child is lying and scold him or her at the counter.

Make a copy of this form for every person or couple in your group. Each week, use the 1–2–3 chart to record at least three attempts to reach the group member—"NA" if there was no answer, "B" if the line was busy, "LM" if you left a message, and "X" when you were able to speak with him or her. Record the person's circumstances, feelings, questions, and ideas in the space labeled "Notes"; refer back to this information the next time you call.

Name(s): ____ *Phone:* ________–__________

Week 1	1	2	3		Week 7	1	2	3
Notes:					Notes:			

Week 2	1	2	3		Week 8	1	2	3
Notes:					Notes:			

Week 3	1	2	3		Week 9	1	2	3
Notes:					Notes:			

Week 4	1	2	3		Week 10	1	2	3
Notes:					Notes:			

Week 5	1	2	3		Week 11	1	2	3
Notes:					Notes:			

Week 6	1	2	3		Week 12	1	2	3
Notes:					Notes:			

Name: ____ Phone: _________–___________

Address: ____

Job (company/title): ____ Years Saved: _______

Spouse: ______________________________ Children (with ages): ________________________

____

Name: ____ Phone: _________–___________

Address: ____

Job (company/title): ____ Years Saved: _______

Spouse: ______________________________ Children (with ages): ________________________

____

Name: ____ Phone: _________–___________

Address: ____

Job (company/title): ____ Years Saved: _______

Spouse: ______________________________ Children (with ages): ________________________

____

Name: ____ Phone: _________–___________

Address: ____

Job (company/title): ____ Years Saved: _______

Spouse: ______________________________ Children (with ages): ________________________

____

Name: ____ Phone: _________–___________

Address: ____

Job (company/title): ____ Years Saved: _______

Spouse: ______________________________ Children (with ages): ________________________

____

Group Member Information

Name: ____ Phone: _______–__________

Address: ____

Job (company/title): _________________________________ Years Saved: _______

Spouse: _____________________ Children (with ages): ___________________

____

Name: ____ Phone: _______–__________

Address: ____

Job (company/title): _________________________________ Years Saved: _______

Spouse: _____________________ Children (with ages): ___________________

____

Name: ____ Phone: _______–__________

Address: ____

Job (company/title): _________________________________ Years Saved: _______

Spouse: _____________________ Children (with ages): ___________________

____

Name: ____ Phone: _______–__________

Address: ____

Job (company/title): _________________________________ Years Saved: _______

Spouse: _____________________ Children (with ages): ___________________

____

Name: ____ Phone: _______–__________

Address: ____

Job (company/title): _________________________________ Years Saved: _______

Spouse: _____________________ Children (with ages): ___________________

____

Name: ____ Phone: _______–__________

Address: ____

Job (company/title): ____ Years Saved: _______

Spouse: ____________________________ Children (with ages): _________________________

____

Name: ____ Phone: _______–__________

Address: ____

Job (company/title): ____ Years Saved: _______

Spouse: ____________________________ Children (with ages): _________________________

____

Name: ____ Phone: _______–__________

Address: ____

Job (company/title): ____ Years Saved: _______

Spouse: ____________________________ Children (with ages): _________________________

____

Name: ____ Phone: _______–__________

Address: ____

Job (company/title): ____ Years Saved: _______

Spouse: ____________________________ Children (with ages): _________________________

____

Name: ____ Phone: _______–__________

Address: ____

Job (company/title): ____ Years Saved: _______

Spouse: ____________________________ Children (with ages): _________________________

____

Name: _______________________________________ Phone: _______–_________

Address: ____

Job (company/title): _______________________________ Years Saved: ______

Spouse: ____________________ Children (with ages): __________________

____

Name: _______________________________________ Phone: _______–_________

Address: ____

Job (company/title): _______________________________ Years Saved: ______

Spouse: ____________________ Children (with ages): __________________

____

Name: _______________________________________ Phone: _______–_________

Address: ____

Job (company/title): _______________________________ Years Saved: ______

Spouse: ____________________ Children (with ages): __________________

____

Name: _______________________________________ Phone: _______–_________

Address: ____

Job (company/title): _______________________________ Years Saved: ______

Spouse: ____________________ Children (with ages): __________________

____

Name: _______________________________________ Phone: _______–_________

Address: ____

Job (company/title): _______________________________ Years Saved: ______

Spouse: ____________________ Children (with ages): __________________

____

Notes